HEREFORD
Then & Now

by Derek Foxton

HEREFORD
Then . . . .

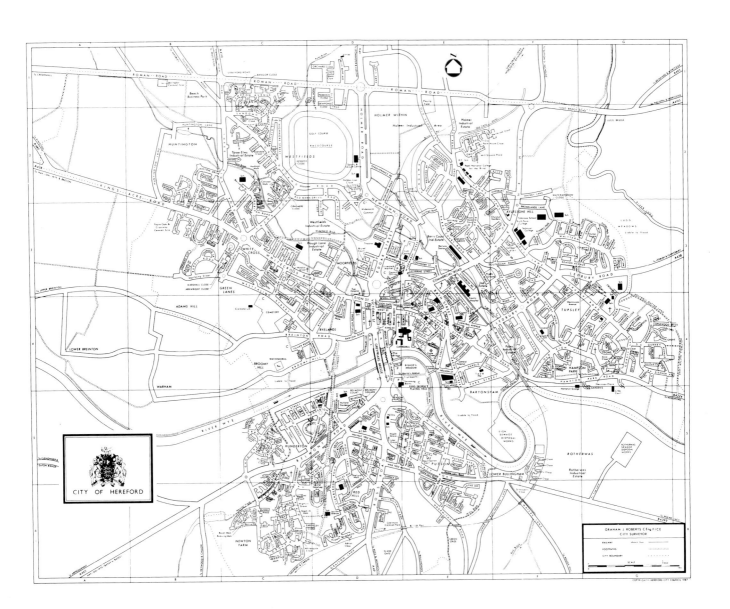

Published by
Derek Foxton
15a Commercial Street
Hereford
HR1 2DE
Telephone: 0432 269666

ISBN 0 9514081 0 0

Designed and produced by
Amber Graphics
Bideford House
Church Lane
Ledbury
Herefordshire
HR8 1DW

Printed by
The Amadeus Press Ltd., Huddersfield

Introduction

Following the publication of my book — *Hereford in Old Picture Postcards* — which is now out of print, I have collected and been given many more hundreds of old picture postcards and photographs of Hereford, most of which have never been published before. They are a valuable source of information and interest. This City which is full of history has a changing face which is largely un-recorded.

Since my school days, I have had an interest in photography and was helped in my school vacations by Derek Evans, F.R.P.S., a well known professional photographer, in his old studio in Broad Street. He even paid me pocket money! During my university life in London, I found time to act as a part-time freelance photographer for the Beaverbrook Newspaper Group. During those years, the Hereford Times, then in Maylord Street, occasionally risked their page 3 pictures in my hands.

There are now several books on Hereford in old pictures and all offer something different. However, many of my patients suggested a book comparing the past and present and I accepted this challenge. It has proved to be a very interesting exercise, but also frustrating at times. Many of the good old views are impossible to photograph today, often because of extensive tree growth.

During the summer months several public events take place in the City and I have tried to use these to add interest to otherwise rather plain views. In many photographs, I have included the motor car and bus, since in fifty or one hundred years' time our future generations can look at our transport with interest, just as we gaze at the horse drawn carriages and carts in the old pictures throughout this book.

In 1988 the City Council closed St. Peter Street and Commercial Street to all traffic. The old road surface and pavements were removed and paved in brick. This created a problem for the author, and the most recent photographs were taken in October to show the success of the scheme. In early November, works were continuing in Commercial Street.

With regard to the old pictures, in some cases the original postcards and photographs I have used have been decidedly faded sepia prints and unfortunately have not been ideal subjects for reproduction. However, I have included them for their unique historic content rather than for their photographic quality.

Most of the postcards have been reproduced from glass plate negatives which were the product of large wooden bodied cameras, extremely wide angle lenses, a tripod and a black hood under which the photographer put his head. It was possible with these cameras to adjust the two ends to compensate for the less than vertical appearance of buildings caused by the wide angle lens. Unfortunately, this facility is not available on today's small hand-held, electronic, automatic reflex cameras, and in some instances there is a slight distortion in the vertical plane on the modern photographs. It does not mean that the buildings have started to change shape since Edwardian times!

I hope that this book will be of wide interest to present day readers and eventually provide some historical reference for our future generations. Already the reader will be able to see the tragic loss of some interesting old buildings.

I give my thanks to the following (not in order of merit): Mr. R. A. Banks of Kington, the Francis Frith Collection in Andover, The Dean and Chapter of Hereford Cathedral, The Hereford City Council for use of their city map, Mr. Lance Marshall of the Royal National College for the Blind and Visually Handicapped, Father Hugh Broad and The Rev. Richard Heading.

Also, I am grateful to the following for help and advice: Mr. Basil Butcher, Mr. Ron Shoesmith, Miss Anne Sandford, Peter Norman at Edwin John Photography, The County Records Office and staff, The City Library Reference Section, Mr. Harold Morgan, Mr. David Postle and finally to my wife Maria, daughters Dominique and Jessica, for enduring many hours of household disruption.

Derek Foxton
November 1988

Opposite top: The See of Hereford is one of the oldest in England. It was 676 when Bishop Putta was given a plot of land in Hereford on which to build a church. The present stone building dates from the Normans and is the central, most dominant feature of the City. It was built using a local sandstone and has been restored over the years. The nave is one arch short following the collapse of the west front tower 200 years ago.

Opposite bottom: The scaffolding which has been present for many years is now being removed. An appeal for one million pounds was launched by patrons Prince Charles and Princess Diana in 1985. The target has now almost been reached. The recently restored pinnacle can be clearly seen.

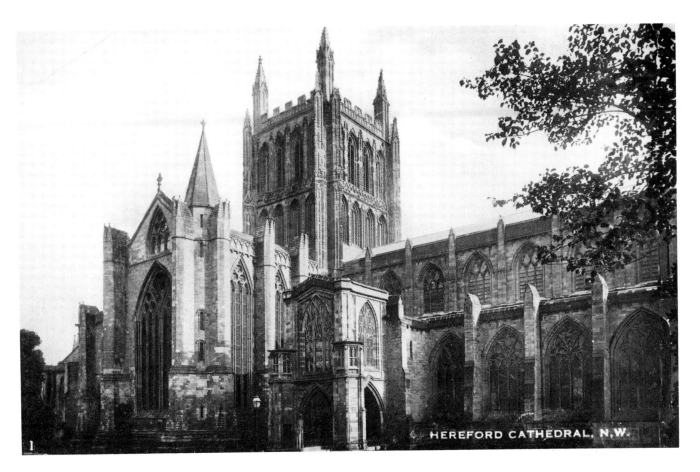

HEREFORD CATHEDRAL, N.W.

Early aerial photographs of Hereford are of special interest This shows a view of the river and Cathedral taken about 1920. The Bishops Meadows are grazing land and the Castle Green has some young trees. Virtually the whole of the City Centre is visible. The bowling area on the castle green is just defined and has no protective fence. It was opened in 1908 by Councillor J. Mitchell.

This photograph was taken during the spring of 1988 in very poor weather by the author. However it does show several major changes — the tennis courts and putting green on the Bishops Meadow, the new ring road, the cider storage vats at H.P. Bulmer and the major shopping developments of Tesco and Maylord Orchards.

This is the view from the top of the Cathedral Tower with Broad Street on the left and All Saints Church in the centre. The dome is on St. Francis Xavier's Church roof. Note the wide open areas behind the church spire. The gas works at Mortimer Road, opened in 1873, are visible to the right of centre line.

Many of the early features remain in the picture today. However, the intense building programme of recent years can be seen. The features of interest are — Bulmers Cider large storage vats, the roof lines of Tesco supermarket, the Cattlemarket, and Maylord Orchards shopping development. In the middle can be seen the back of Littlewoods and Marks and Spencer stores. The British Telecom building in Church Street is seen near the lower border.

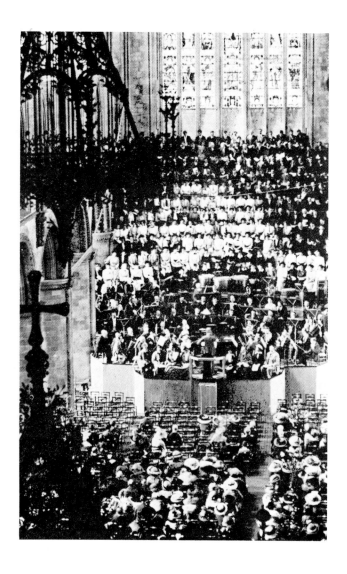

The Hereford Three Choirs Music Festival in 1912 photographed from a gallery high up in the tower. In this year Elgar composed the suite from the Crown of India which had its first performance here. Many of Elgar's compositions were first performed at the Three Choirs Festival during his lifetime. The conductor was G. S. Sinclair age 48. In 1912 the Festival was 185 years old.

This photograph was taken at ground level by the author during the organ recital by David Briggs at the opening service for the 1988 Festival. The scene has changed very little over the last 76 years. The empty seats await the civic and clerical heads of the three counties of Herefordshire, Gloucestershire and Worcestershire. The Conductor is Roy Massey age 53. This picture is reproduced by kind permission of the Dean and Chapter of Hereford Cathedral.

High Town about 1920 with the motor taxis awaiting their fares. The steeple on top of All Saints Church is undergoing repairs. Note the buildings to the left of the Butter Market Hall. They were demolished in 1928 to make way for a new Lloyds Bank. The Butter Market Hall was opened on 10th October 1860. The London City and Midland Bank occupied the High Street corner. The manager was Mr. Roland Edwards. High Town was not always a wide open area. A superb black and white half-timbered Market Hall stood on oak pillars in the middle but was sadly demolished in 1862, and a row of old houses called Butchers Row adjoined the Old House.

The author found the view all through the summer and autumn 1988 was blocked by the contractors who paved St. Peter Street and Commercial Street. Visitors today can see that the results were worth waiting for. Dark coloured paving slabs are laid in the positions of the old oak pillars of the Market Hall, and there is also an engraved stone on the eastern edge of this site.

This must be the second most popular postcard view of Hereford. Every face of the old house, built in 1621, is found on early picture postcards. The hut is one of two used by the City's cabbies. Judging by the long costumes worn, the postcard must date to the early years after the turn of the century.

During the 1988 carnival week the city museum brought out its Hereford-made gipsy caravan. It was recently restored by one of its original carpenters. Here it is being used by the Association for the Promotion of Herefordshire to give advice and distribute leaflets.

St. Peter Street about 1938 showing traffic pointing in both directions. This road was the exit from the city centre towards Ledbury and Fownhope. In 1928 the Old House was given to the City by Lloyds Bank who had occupied it for many years.

During the summer and autumn of 1988 the area was pedestrianised and re-surfaced with paving bricks. This photograph shows part of the completed works. The road is closed to all traffic except for delivery and the disabled. The mature trees now partly obscure the Old House.

The City and County Dining Rooms where Mr. Henry Jones was the manager had perhaps the prime site in the City Centre, with one side facing High Town and the other the Old House. The banners proclaim God Save the King. The date and occasion are unknown but it could possibly be the Coronation of King George V. The ladies are wearing full length costumes.

The building has been carefully restored after it ceased to be the Tabbard Inn, and is now occupied by a Building Society in a predominantly shopping area.

The south side of High Town before the First World War clearly shows several shop window displays. Gardners at No. 20 were milliners, Mason a music warehouse and sub-post office. Note the replica pipe organ on the first floor level. The Domestic Bazaar sold glass and china. Next was the Maypole Dairy Co. and finally on the far right, Townsends — optician and bicycle agent. Most of the owners lived above their shops. There is a superb exterior gas lamp outside the Domestic Bazaar. It is possibly Sunday morning, the pedestrians are in their 'best' clothes and are probably on their way to church.

Today, the shops are much larger and double width but the fronts are very simple and far less interesting. Townsends are still in business — the grandsons Tim and Robin now run an office equipment business in Saint Owen Street. The pavement in front of the buildings has recently been re-paved.

High Town in 1907. To the left of the picture shop No. 31 was occupied by Greenlands the house furnishers. Rodgers, next door, were fruiterers. The shop behind the lamp post is the entrance to Rudolph Siever, a Surgeon Dentist. Greenlands also occupy the next two shops in the light coloured building. Many Herefordians still remember the grocers Marchants, who occupied the triple fronted black and white premises.

The scene has changed dramatically. Even the front of Marchant & Matthews old shop, now a part of Littlewoods, has been moved. Many Herefordians will remember it stored in High Town some twenty years ago. Today such partial demolition would probably not be allowed. The new fronts of Marks and Spencer, and Littlewoods have lost a lot of the old City character.

The souvenir seller touring the fairground has an admiring audience of children who have possibly spent all their pocket money. In the background can be seen the sign of Heins music shop.

The balloon seller provides a colourful picture and like her predecessor, walks the length and breadth of the fair. The buildings have changed, but the name Heins lives on with Nigel Heins, a journalist for the Hereford Times and his father, a partly retired local Estate Agent.

Opposite top: The City of Hereford has to allow an annual street fair in the month of May, according to a charter by Henry I to the Bishop of Hereford. In 1838 an Act of Parliament gave control of the fair to the citizens, and the Bishop was compensated by an annual payment of 12½ bushels of wheat. The motive power for the roundabouts and supply of electricity was from a showman's traction engine. One is seen here in the centre of High Town. The building at the top left was occupied by the printers Jakeman and Carver.

Opposite bottom: The modern fair still incorporates many of the old roundabouts, as well as many stomach-shaking new ideas.

St. Peter's Square about 1930's and the heyday of the bus, long before car ownership was widespread. The Shire Hall was erected in 1815 at a cost of £52,000 and opened in 1817. Inside were the County Hall, the Courts of Law apartments for the Judges and Grand Jury. On the granite pedestal is a statue of Sir George Cornewall Lewis M.P. for Hereford 1847-1852, Chancellor of the Exchequer 1855-1858 and Home Secretary 1859-1860. He died in 1863. The Herefordshire War Memorial was unveiled on October 7th 1922 by Col. Drage and committed to the Corporation of Hereford by the Colonel of the Herefordshire Regiment, Col. Scobie C.B. The names of the fallen were inscribed in a book to be kept by the Dean and Chapter in the Cathedral. The Council minutes dated 10th March 1922 directed that a gas lamp and horse trough had to be removed to make way for the memorial.

This mid-summer photograph shows the re-paving and alterations to the memorial in progress. The new flower beds have been planted while the base of the memorial unfortunately is used as a resting place. The new City Hopper buses can be seen to the left.

St. Peter's Square and St Owen's Street. The style of the motor cars indicates that it is about 1937. The Town Hall had its foundation stone laid by HRH Princess Henry of Battenburg on 13th May 1902 when Edward Bosley was the Mayor. It stands high above the adjacent buildings which are now virtually all listed.

Today nearly every building remains the same. Here the Mayor and Mayoress of Hereford, Councillor Basil Baldwin and his wife Sylvia, ride in a vintage Alvis car driven by David Moruzzi at the head of the City carnival.

The corner shop of T. Lindsey-Price in St. Peter Street and Offa Street during the year 1909.
He sold carpets, furniture, linoleum and curtains. Previously, in 1905 Maddox, a house furnisher,
had occupied this shop. In 1914 Lindsey Price moved into larger premises at 16 & 17 Commercial
Street. They closed down in 1985.

The small panes of glass in the upstairs windows have been replaced with large sheets of glass.
Sunderland & Co, Estate Agents, now occupy the premises.

22

This secret City Centre retreat is behind a house opposite the Town Hall. It was taken in 1913 at the rear of "Cliftonia" which was occupied by Mr. and Mrs. Barter, who are seen seated in their garden.

The house which has been empty for nearly two years awaits alteration and renovation by builders. Planning permission has been sought to convert it into a hotel. It has in recent years been used by Hattons, a fishing tackle manufacturer and retailer, and then for a short period by the Hereford Observer advertising weekly. The house is a Grade II listed building.

The street is very quiet, the traffic is now only allowed one way and the scaffolding over the Town Hall entrance has just gone. The last time such a huge crowd was here was on the Royal Visit by the Queen and the Duke of Edinburgh on December 10th 1987.

Opposite: The scene in front of the Town Hall May 10th 1910. The proclamation of King George V was read in the presence of the Mayor (Mr Walter Pilley), Sir James Rankin, M.P. (Chief Steward), Mr. J. S. Arkwright, M.P., Members of the Corporation, Magistrates and other prominent citizens, representatives of the Hereford-shire Regiment and the school children. Note all the summer hats.

The Young Women's Christian Association and Percival Hall in St. Owen's Street photographed probably on Empire Day about 1922. This picture postcard is marked with a cross on the front and inscribed on the reverse 'Love from Alice'. The lady Superintendent was Mrs. Bridgewater.

In 1986 a small shopping mews development was completed next door to the YWCA, which itself remains unaltered. The new car parking arrangement in the street seems to have provided drivers with a slight alignment problem.

A recruiting parade in St. Ethelbert Street during 1914. The Castle Pool Hotel is in the background but appears very faint. No doubt the recruits joined the Herefordshire Regiment and fought in the trenches. This postcard has a cross marked and on the reverse it is dated 26th September 1914 and signed 'Wilf'.

St. Ethelbert Street is now in a conservation area and no new houses have been built this century. Today the street has changed from its residential status to partial retail use at its St. Owen's Street junction.

This is High Street with the Old House just visible in the distance. All through traffic used this narrow road until the opening of the inner ring road on December 11th 1968. The shops are closed so it is probably a Sunday. The trading sign 'Singers' refers to the popular sewing machine still in use today.

The 1988 City carnival organised by the Hereford and District Chamber of Commerce brought the City Centre to a standstill. The procession gets bigger and better each year.

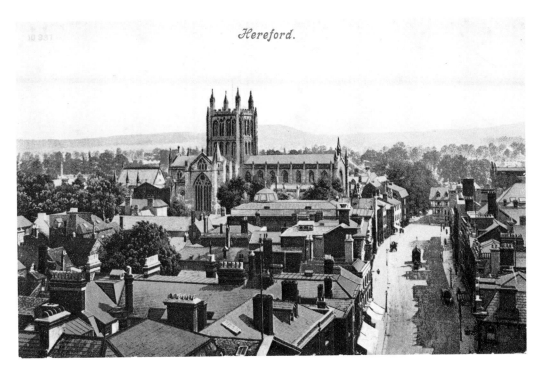

A panorama from All Saints Church tower shows Broad Street and a profusion of chimney pots. The Cathedral is very dominant on the skyline. At the far end of Broad Street note the buildings in front of the west end of the Cathedral. The cabbies' hut stands alone in the street.

This photograph of the 1988 May Fair was taken at night with the camera held by hand and a long exposure. The Burton building and Barclays Bank are featured in the foreground, while the big wheel rotates in a maze of lights in the distance. The Cathedral is picked out by the flood lighting around it.

Today the view from this position has remained very much the same. Only in the far distance have the buildings been replaced with late 20th century designs which are not in keeping with the character of the ancient City. The car number plates were prefixed with the letter F after August 1988. The old hut has been removed to Bishops Meadows where it is used by Council attendants for the issuing of tickets and golf clubs.

Opposite: A view of Broad Street before the turn of the century shows a horse drawn two-wheeled cart. The hut in the middle of the street was a shelter used by the cabbies for rest and dry storage for hay. A stone water trough was near the entrance to the Catholic Church on the right. Before the opening of the Edgar Street cattle market, an open market was held all along Broad Street every Wednesday.

This is a rare glimpse looking south along Broad Street. The two horse-drawn vehicles and one hand cart indicate a busy day in the street. The gas lamps are alight. The majestic front of the Green Dragon Hotel dominates the view. Note the statue on top of the Old Corn Exchange next to the library.

During the 1988 carnival on Saturday evening of 11th July, the streets were closed and all motor vehicles removed. Crowd protection barriers were erected for the cycle racing or *Kermisse*. The Green Dragon is temporarily hidden by the scaffolding while it is repainted. Note the new buildings past the hotel.

Hogben Bros who sold hats, linen and fabrics were on the corner of Broad Street and Eign Street. This was a very good commercial position in the heart of the City Centre.

For many years the firm Mac Fisheries occupied this site. The present occupant is F. Hinds, a jewellery shop.

KING'S HEAD HOTEL, HEREFORD.

This superb photographic postcard view of the Kings Head Hotel was posted in 1907 and no doubt many Herefordians will remember this building. The landlord in 1907 was Alfred Willis.

What a pity the old building was demolished. The modern prefabricated facia does not do any justice to the City. Fortunately, listed building orders now prevent the loss of many such buildings. Future generations will judge whether or not this was a 1970's act of vandalism.

The City Arms Hotel was originally built by the Duke of Norfolk as his town house about 1785. It became a hotel in mid-Victorian times, quite imposing and comfortable. During its last years it was a Trust House Forte Hotel. This ultra wide angle photograph gives a rare glimpse into East Street.

When the hotel closed it was purchased by Barclays Bank, who all but demolished the building. Only a small half-timbered rear room and the front walls remained so to the observer it is difficult to appreciate the change. Note the extension in the same style in East Street.

The start of the Hereford Light Car Trials on Monday August 29th 1904. No. 20 is a 6 h.p. Light Wolsley. The motoring press noted the addition of an oil drip tray beneath the engine to protect it from dust and dirt thrown up by the wheels. This photograph reproduced by kind permission of Mr. R. A. Banks of Kington was taken by his father in Broad Street outside Oswins and the Mitre Hotel. This car did exceptionally well. It travelled a different route of over 100 miles non-stop each day for six days — a total of 600 miles.

Here is the start of the first full re-enactment of the trials on Monday 29th August 1988, organised by the Midlands Section of the Veteran Car Club. It was opened by the Mayor, Cllr.Basil Baldwin. On the original event the route for each day was a lap of 50 miles which was covered twice. However this year only one lap was driven so that the total mileage was 300. No. 1 is a Santler-Malvernia of 1894, made in Malvern and is recorded as the oldest British made motor car still running.

KEMBLE THEATRE, HEREFORD

This postcard photograph taken about 1920 of the Kemble Theatre shows what a magnificent building it was. The building was originally the Corn Exchange with a Bath stone front built in 1857 and a tower containing the illuminated clock. It cost £3,580, which was raised by subscription. It was enlarged in 1911 by adding a public hall and theatre at a cost of £5,000. It seated 1,000 people.

Today only the name survives on a round wall plaque, which reads "Site of the Corn Exchange 1857-1950. Demolished in 1963".

The main Post Office in the City is in Broad Street. It has an interesting stone facia with some ecclesiastical features. Lined up in front are the staff with the manager, Samuel Ilsey. Nine workers are in tunics without a tie and eight with winged collars and ties. The postmaster is sixth from the right with a beard and rolled umbrella. The sign behind the men indicates separate boxes for letters and newspapers.

The eight steps up to the entrance remain, and are a barrier to the disabled who no doubt use St. Peter's Square Post Office. The new sign states that the steps must be kept clear at all times. The post box is now on the outside wall, together with a hanging sign and alarm system bell box. The building is now over 100 years old.

The old Residence Private Hotel at the corner of King Street and Broad Street looks rather out of place in such a central area. It was originally a residence for a canon of the Cathedral and is a fine looking Victorian structure with some gothic influence.

Today we see three estate agents under the same roof. In 1988 alone, we have seen a very large increase in house prices. The change of architecture is stunning and a contrast to the ancient Cathedral opposite.

This is King Street in October 1909. Looking west, it shows two mounted policemen leading an army parade with a military band. Behind the horses, just visible in the background, is the St. Nicholas Church tower which was erected in 1842. The Church was originally on a site at the top of Bridge Street before being moved to its present position.

A 1988 parade but going the other way. Most of the buildings on the right side are unchanged, while the new Bernard Thorpe building, Thorpe House, dominates the corner.

King Street looking towards the Cathedral in 1905. The majority of buildings visible are residential, except for the Spread Eagle near the far end and a fruiterer and tailor to the right edge. In between are accountants, auctioneers and architects who lived upstairs above their businesses. Just visible is the scaffolding on the Cathedral west front. In 1786, the western tower, 135 feet high, which was partly of Norman origin, collapsed. The new front designed by James Wyatt was erected in 1788, but shortened the nave by 15 feet. Part of the new front, designed by Oldred Scott, can be seen.

The street is now a busy commercial area and most buildings except solicitors, T. A. Matthews, have had shop fronts inserted. At present the majority of premises are occupied by estate agents.

The Orange Tree Inn in King Street at the turn of the century. This superb postcard features four horses showing their fine display of brass and the brake wagon with its fifteen male occupants. The landlord at the time was George Barnham. The Orange Tree was built in the seventeenth century as a rectory for Saint Nicholas Church. Next door on the right is the entrance to the famous photographer Ladmore and Son.

The front of the Inn has been altered since the turn of the century. Without this comparison it would be difficult to decide which was the original. However, the later additions have created an attractive front. The present landlord, retired dental technician John Duggan, said that the oak panelling at the back of the lounge bar is reputed to have come from the Greyfriars Monastery.

This postcard view of Bridge Street was posted in August 1913. It shows a horse-drawn hay wagon on its way to market. The Wye bridge is in the foreground. The white house on the left was called Wye Bridge House, where Mrs. Lane lived. Next door was Jordan the boat builder. The front of the Black Lion, an agricultural inn, can be seen. Along this side of the street were six solicitors. The shop on the right side next to the bridge was Henry Slann, a fruiterer.

Today all the buildings on the west side (left) remain, though on the east side there are new premises, originally built by Sullys for their motor showroom. An upper floor showroom has been added in recent years.

Wye Terrace next to the old bridge has one of the best views of the river in Hereford. Some of the houses have internal exposed timber framing. When the river is very high, the gardens and ground floors are flooded. Perhaps that is the reason for such healthy growth in the gardens!

Today, during the summer months, the visitor has to stop and look between the trees to view the Terrace. The houses, however, still retain their river views.

This must be the most popular postcard view of Hereford, and is how most people remember the City. The stone bridge, built about 1490, is the oldest over the River Wye. In the foreground are the boats belonging to Jordans boat yard. The photographer was next to the terminus of the old horse-drawn tramway to Abergavenny.

The new bridge frames this 1988 view of the old bridge. The showroom adjacent to the bridge with the name of Mead & Tomkinson was built in the 1920's. The children engage in the ancient sport of fishing.

This 1920's picture postcard of the old bridge was taken adjacent to the site of an early ford crossing which, it is thought, the Romans used. This was the only bridge over the Wye until 1597, when the Ross-on-Wye Wilton bridge was built. In 1645 the third arch from the north bank was demolished as a defence against the Scots army.

In 1988 the old bridge is still in use

This large house which dates from early Victorian times stands on the river bank, two hundred yards upstream from the old Wye bridge. According to sale documents dated 1885 for the house, its land extended past the rowing club upstream, to Barton Road in the north and to Wye Terrace downstream. Nearby is the lost site of the old Greyfriars Monastery. During recent excavations, while digging foundations for an extension to a house in Greyfriars Avenue, some buried human remains were found. They are thought to be from the burial ground attached to the monastery.

About 1970 an extension was built for the Greyfriars Restaurant. Its floor height is just above the level of more recent floods. It is sad to note that the small semi-circular window in the attic has lost its intricate tracery. Note that the right side chimney pot has been re-built.

This picture of the regatta was taken about 1908. It looks as if there were plenty of hospitality available in the marquees along the bank. The coxed fours are near the finish. The steeple of All Saints appears directly behind the tower of St. Nicholas Church.

The 1988 raft race proved less of an attraction to spectators, but the competitors did manage to raise many thousands of pounds for charity in the county. In 1987 the Committee for Herefordshire Amateur Rafters raised £63,000. The rafts are paddled from Hay-on-Wye to Chepstow over three days in early May.

The Hereford Infirmary photographed in 1910. This building dates back to March 1776 and was built on land donated by the Earl of Oxford. In 1928 it was reported that there were eleven wards and two isolation wards. The Hospital could accommodate 125 patients, 50 male, 50 female and 25 children. It was supported by subscriptions.

Now called the General Hospital, it is seen in its final expanded form. It has been recently reported that a new district general hospital will be built at Burghill. It will cost forty-two million pounds and will not be completed until the mid-1990's.

The Cathedral has always been the postcard photographer's favourite subject. This view, framed by trees, is from the Bartonsham Meadows. It is early spring and the College of Art can also be seen. The Queen Victoria Diamond Jubilee suspension bridge over the River Wye was built in 1898 at a cost of £1200.

In the mid-summer of 1988, the meadow flowers are out and the tree on the left has reached maturity. Note the children in the middle of the river which is at a summer low.

The Cathedral, College of Art and River Wye about 1925. The white faced longhorn Hereford cattle graze and drink along the Wye banks. The Hereford Herd Book Society in East Street is the world wide centre for recording the pedigree in every aspect. The Principal of the Science and Art College was Henry Baynton.

The old College buildings are now used for storage and meetings by the canoeing club. On both banks the trees have grown and on the Bishops Meadows an avenue of trees planted in 1937 has matured. The Meadows were vested in Hereford Corporation as a public space and playing field in perpetuity by the Right Reverend John Percival D.D., Lord Bishop of Hereford, who gave the leasehold in 1914, and The Right Reverend Charles Lisle Carr D.D., who gave the freehold in 1937. A tablet to commemorate this was unveiled near the Victoria Bridge by H.M. Queen Mary on 29th July 1937.

The Castle Green, site of the Hereford Castle, was a popular spot on Sundays in Victorian and Edwardian times. This picture, taken just before the First World War, shows several families wearing their Sunday-best clothes. The cannons at the foot of the Nelson Monument can be seen. It looks as if the City Corporation Parks Department have recently planted trees on the far side. The green was first used as a public park in 1753. The column is 60 feet high and erected in commemoration of Lord Nelson, who was killed at Trafalgar in 1805.

Today the green is still a popular recreation area. The bowling green now dominates the southern part and is protected by a solid hedge. The trees round the perimeter have now fully matured. One of the old cannons, Roaring Meg, was used at the siege of Goodrich Castle. All the remaining cannons reputedly used in the 1645 siege of the City by the Parliamentarians are now at the Churchill Gardens.

Eign Street in 1906 with the spires of All Saints Church on the left and St. Peter's in the centre. The children are very smartly dressed but the occasion is not known. The street carried traffic in both directions.

Today the view is not very impressive, as the trees planted some eighteen years ago have grown. It is difficult to imagine how large vehicles could travel in opposite directions and pass parked cars.

Eign Street decorations celebrating Empire Day in 1906. The large flags almost form an arch across Eign Street. This view looking to the east shows Clarksons and Stewart's — Peoples Stores with a board advertising Gilbys wines and spirits. Next door is Thackways, the tobacconist. Seven shops further on is Jennings, the saddler.

The street is now completely free of motorised traffic — it was pedestrianised some eighteen years ago. Of the shops in the earlier photograph, only Jennings are left. They have been in business since the early 1850's.

This rather fuzzy Wilson and Phillips postcard dates no later than 1904 and shows T. A. King's Victoria Marble and Stone Works at the junction of Eign Street and Victoria Street. A photograph in a 1907 catalogue for this business describes them as the Hereford Motor Co. and clearly shows a large showroom where the stone memorials are. They sold a wide range of cars from Daimler to Rolls Royce. The whole building was demolished in 1967.

Victoria Street today is a part of the City inner ring road. A pedestrian underpass marks the site of the old buildings. Above the cyclists, a part of the medieval City wall can be seen. In the underpass, the extent of the ancient City ditch found during excavations is marked in tiles on one wall. Here we see an attempt by the regulars of the Moorfields Inn to enter the Guinness Book of Records. They have linked some 20 bicycles together for a ride to Mordiford and back with suitable stops on route.

A view into Commercial Street from High Town about 1928. The Georgian building to the left was 5 Commercial Street and used as the Judges' lodgings. This building was demolished to make way for the Odeon Cinema in 1937. The road traffic moved quite freely in both directions.

This view taken in 1988 shows the never ending changes that take place. The new front of Maylord Orchards can be seen on the left while the road is up in preparation for re-paving.

This picture of Commercial Street and Gomond Street was taken about 50 years ago by Mr. Percy Pritchard A.R.P.S. The empty shop formerly occupied by Workmans awaits a new tenant. They were described as general merchants and ironmongers. Across Gomond Street is seen the Ministry of Labour Employment Exchange. The date stone high up on this building in Gomond Street is 1910.

This photograph taken on a very dull day, shows the new Maylord Orchards frontage. The Laura Ashley shop has lost its Edwardian ironwork on the first floor window balconies, whilst its new shop front has been praised as an example of excellent design. The road at the time of writing is in the process of being re-paved.

This is the north side of Commercial Street looking towards Commercial Square. The shop on the left is William Price, the newsagent, with tobacconist Fred Turke next door. In the middle distance can be seen the twin ends of The Trinity Hospital (sometimes known as Kerry's Hospital).

The water board has renewed its water main along the street leaving a temporary scar. The window frames above the shop on the left remain in what is now the charity shop. Further along can be seen the two dormer windows above Chadds department store. A recent survey by the City Archaeological Committee has reported that the rear part of the Chadds building adjacent to Preece's Passage is at least one hundred years older than the famous Old House.

This photograph was taken about 1910 before the builders had completed work. It opened as the Board of Trade Labour Exchange and replaced a small timber-framed building occupied by Mary Wright, who sold glass and china.

The new Laura Ashley shop front is one modern design which does justice to the building. It has recently been awarded a plaque by the Conservation Advisory Committee.

Here is a glimpse of the extensive range of hardware goods sold in Harding Brothers shop in Commercial Street. They had an iron foundry in Bath Street and further shops at 9 and 30 Union Street plus a warehouse in the Cattle Market. The Commercial Street building was demolished in 1964 to make way for Tesco.

Commercial Street was closed to through traffic in May 1988. The Tesco architects left Hereford with this design, which is now occupied by Macdonalds. The contrast in shop front design is startling. The passageway through to Union Street is visible to the right.

Hatton and Co. occupied both these shops in Commercial Street for very many years. They were watchmakers, gold and silversmiths. Next door to the right, Liptons — the grocers, can just be seen.

Both the old buildings have gone and been replaced by the new premises of the National Westminster Bank, who once traded near this spot over 130 years ago, and Pickfords Travel Agents.

COMMERCIAL SQUARE, HEREFORD

2055

Commercial Square about 50 years ago showing a rare glimpse into both Commercial Street and Union Street. The roundabout was planted and tended by the City Corporation. The site of the old City gate — Bysters Gate, would have been near the Kerry Arms and its adjacent City wall was started in 1298.

Several features of the 1980's are present here. The pedestrian refuge in the centre of Commercial Road was erected in 1988, while the 'E' registration on the car indicates 1987 or 1988. The post box has been moved away from the road junction.

To the left of this photograph is Blueschool Street and to the right is Bath Street. The view along Commercial Road was taken from a first floor window in the Kerry Arms Hotel. The Sanitary Laundry is on the left of the picture while Lewis Smith, the chemist is on the right where it still is today. This postcard, reproduced with permission of the Francis Frith Collection, was taken in the early 1950's.

The road junction is now part of the City Inner Ring Road which was opened in 1968. The Sanitary Laundry building was demolished as well as the buildings this side of it to make space for the dual carriageway. The new 'Hopper' bus is on its way to Tupsley.

FESTIVAL DECORATIONS — COMMERCIAL ROAD. F.PREECE .PHOTO!

A view of Commercial Road in September 1906 towards the Kerry Arms Hotel. The huge decorative twin arch surmounted by the City coat of arms, was erected across Commercial Road every third year just before the start of the Hereford Three Choirs Festival held in mid-September. Behind the trees to the left is Greenland's furniture depository, while to the right the entrance to Monkmore Street can be seen with the Great Western Inn on the corner. A similar arch was erected in Broad Street near the Green Dragon Hotel.

The view today without the arches is somewhat similar and the new buildings clearly seen. The tall building to the left is now I. & J. Brown's antique showroom and restoration workshops, while the Franklin Barnes corner building dominates the right of Commercial Square.

A tree-lined Commercial Road about 1905 with a passing school parade. Nothing is known about this event. The name on the shop front reads J. J. Bennett, who was a butcher.

The same view in 1988 reveals that a soft furnishing shop has replaced the butcher. The tall building in the background, built about 1899, was Greenlands Depository. It is now an antiques shop, I. & J. Brown.

Here we are in the middle of Commercial Road looking towards the north-east and the junction with Monkmoor Street. The row of shops included a taxidermist, bicycle agent, a servants' registry and bootmaker. The Great Western Inn is visible on the far side of the road junction.

The buildings remain, even if the chimney pots do not. The change of use of all the buildings can be seen. The Great Western is now no longer an inn, but a Chinese restaurant.

Barrs Court Station about 1908. The railway line from Shrewsbury to Hereford Barrs Court was opened in 1853. This large building was opened in 1855 as was the line to Ross and Gloucester. In 1861, the line to Worcester was opened while the line to Hay and Brecon took another three years. The line from Newport, which previously ran to Hereford Barton Station, was later rerouted to Barrs Court. The station was thus the centre for all long distance travel. It had a regular horse drawn coach service into the City.

The station buildings are listed and remain very much as they were in 1855. During recent years, road transport has taken a lot of business away from the railways and the total number of employees is a fraction of the number employed in the years prior to the rationalisation of railways masterminded by Dr. Beeching in the 1960's, when many minor routes and small stations were closed.

This is the Rockfield area next to the Hereford and Abergavenny railway line. At the foot of Aylestone Hill, the school children await the Royal Train, which passed through Hereford on Wednesday August 8th 1908 with King Edward VII and Queen Alexandra on board. According to the Great Western timetable for the journey, they stayed at Barrs Court Station from 4.10pm to 4.15pm, to meet the Mayor, Mr. J. Mitchell, who presented the Royal visitors with a loyal address.

The field is now developed as part of the Rockfield Road industrial estate. The author was unable to reproduce the same view. However, the houses are in a Conservation area and remain unaltered.

Aylestone Hill in 1917. A very tranquil scene with no petrol powered vehicle in view. In the distance on the hill a horse drawn cart descends along the centre of the road, while a tricyclist ascends. This prosperous area has many houses which were connected to the city telephone system using the high overhead wires. The turning into Southbank Road can be seen to the middle right, while to the left is Barrs Court Road. Note the gas lamps along the road.

Today the houses retain their original features, even though some windows have modern replacements. The area shown on the photograph is within the Aylestone Hill Conservation Area. The trees have matured, although some have been lost which the City Council has recently replaced.

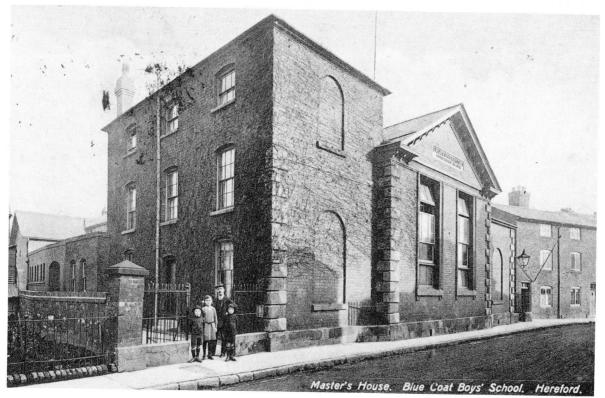

The Bluecoat Boys School in Blueschool Street about 1908. The old street was named Town Ditch, since it ran alongside the ditch just outside the City walls. In 1908 there were 368 scholars and here is the headmaster, Mr. William Caldwell, with his young family. The school was established in 1710, but this building was erected in 1827.

The building still retains the old school name in stone below the gable end. The road is now a dual carriageway and incorporates both Blueschool Street and a part of Maylord Street. In the background Franklin House can be seen.

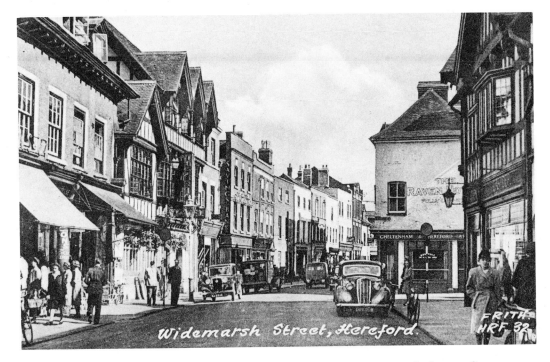

Widemarsh Street about 1946 with traffic travelling two ways and plenty of space to park. To the left is the Mansion House which in January 1907 was the Municipal Surveyors, Gas, Water Works and Rates Office. It had a central entrance up two steps. In July 1907 the Hereford Times published a picture of the two new shops with a drive-through arch. The shop on the left was G. Wright and Son, fruiterers, while on the right was R. J. Jenkins, outfitters. Next door is the Imperial Hotel, a 20th century reproduction half-timbered building. David Garrick was born in 1716 at the Raven Inn and he later became a famous actor. This picture is reproduced by kind permission from the Francis Frith Collection, Andover.

The current view is largely unchanged except that many chimneys were removed during the renovation of the shops in the far distance about four years ago. The cement lorry marks the entrance to Maylord Street and the new shopping centre. The plaque above Black's shop reads 'Formerly the home of William Brewster 1665-1715' whilst the entrance below leads to the Tesco supermarket.

WELLINGTON HOTEL HEREFORD

The Wellington Hotel in Widemarsh Street about 1910. The landlord was Leopold Goffin, who may have tended the high level window-boxes. Note the large gas lamp over the entrance. A long forgotten brewery Salt & Co. advertised their ales.

Instead of being at the corner of a quiet city cross roads, it is now adjacent to the very busy inner ring road which was opened by the local Member of Parliament, David Gibson-Watt, M.C. on December 11th 1968. The building has been recently renovated and a new small replica gas lamp can be seen above the main entrance.

The Black Friars Monastery, Widemarsh Street 1911. Here are the remains of the Dominican Friars monastic buildings which were founded about 1280. The church was consecrated in the presence of Edward III, his son the Black Prince, and three Archbishops. The remains of the refectory and the Prior's house of about 1322 and the 14th century preaching cross are visible.

This shows the sole surviving preaching cross in the county. The ruins were 'restored' during 1962/63, made possible through the generosity of the River Wye Guild.

Conningsby Hospital, once called Red Coat Hospital, is only a short distance from the old Widemarsh Gate. It was erected in 1614 by Sir Thomas Conningsby of Hampton Court and incorporates part of a house of the Knights of St John of Jerusalem dated thirteenth century. In earlier years all the residents wore red coats. This view of the courtyard in 1906 shows the water pump and a resident.

On the author's visit all was quiet with no one in sight. Recent restoration work supervised by Hook-Mason Architectural Partnership has preserved all the ancient features, but given all modern conveniences to the residents.

The date is just after the Great War — a horse drawn delivery wagon trundles slowly through the Newtown Road flood. The Tan Brook frequently flooded the road here. In the distance is the post office with a bakers shop next door. The foreground shows the coal merchants, Albert Baker.

In recent years the local drainage system has been improved so that it has been a long time since the road flooded. The view photographed in heavy rain has remained very much the same.

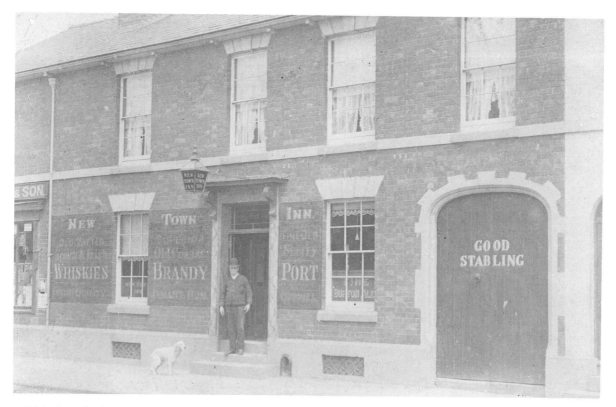

This faded photograph of the Newtown Inn in Newtown Road, Widemarsh shows the landlord Albert Adams in June 1907. To the left can be seen the grocers shop owned by Mr. Hall, who also had a sub-post office. The 'Good Stabling' notice was no doubt to attract visitors coming into town by horse.

The end building is now a private residence, while the old inn has now become the Widemarsh Post Office. The large stable entrance remains. Only just visible is the iron boot scraper on the pavement near the door step. The ground floor windows have enlarged panes of glass.

This postcard was posted in Hereford, August 1912. On the reverse the message reads 'our camp'. There are many dozens of small tents all the way over College Hill. Note the 'vital' beer barrels on the railway truck, but perhaps on their way elsewhere. The military horses can be seen in the field above the railway engine.

Today the view from the Newtown Road railway bridge shows the large college housing estate and pre-fabs which have survived longer than their designed life. The triple towers of Painter Brothers can be seen where many electricity pylons have been assembled. Their most famous structure was the Skylon made for the Festival of Britain 1951.

Memorial Cross, Widemarsh Common, Holmer

This undated postcard is about 1920. The horses are on their way home after delivering a load of timber in the City. The memorial looks very new with fresh flowers on the second step.

It is Sunday, the traffic is light and the new mini roundabout facilitates easier traffic flow at this junction. The roof of the new City Leisure Centre is visible in the distance. The memorial has just been removed and re-erected on the far side of the Widemarsh Common, as seen in the lower picture.

Barton goods yard and engine sheds about 1958. This view from the Barton Road railway bridge towards the Eign Street railway bridge shows a lot of activity. The railways carried most of the nation's freight. This rapidly declined during the following decade and the rails were removed in the 1960's and 1970's. The area became disused for many years. This photograph was taken by Mr. H. B. Priestley who kindly gave permission to reproduce this picture.

The new telephone exchange building was the first to make some use of the old sidings. Later the City Council moved their base from Stonebow Road to Grimmer Road. The latest and most comprehensive development is by J. Sainsbury plc. who have just opened their supermarket.

HOLY TRINITY CHURCH AND VICARAGE HEREFORD.

Holy Trinity Church and Vicarage in White Cross Road on a postcard dated August 1913. Both the church and vicarage look quite new and the trees still young. The Holy Trinity Parish was formed on January 14th 1902 from parts of All Saints, St. John the Baptist, St. Nicholas, Hereford, and Saint Bartholomew, Holmer. The church was erected in 1885 at a cost of £4,800. It is built of red sandstone with freestone dressings.

The trees including the yew have grown. The vicarage garden is in the process of preparation for the 1988 church fete. This picture is published with kind permission of the Rev. Richard Heading.

The Whitecross about 1904 looking eastwards. The steps form a resting place for city walkers as it is about one mile from the centre. There are several stories about its history. The cross marks the spot where food was brought to the City and left for the occupants during the time of an infectious plague in Hereford in 1347. According to Duncomb's history of Hereford, another theory is that when Bishop Thomas de Cantelupe 1275-83, who was travelling towards the City, reached this spot, he heard the Cathedral bells ring out of their own accord.

Today the monument remains in the centre of a busy traffic island. It has a hexagonal base and steps, and was heavily restored in 1864.

Chandos Street in Whitecross about 1925 and not a person in sight. In the street resided Mrs. Kate Volpé, a teacher of music, Alfred Gwatkin, an insurance agent, Arthur Howard, a cycle dealer, Thomas Hiles, a builder and William Robinson, a grocer. The Primitive Methodist Chapel was built in 1909 at a cost of over £3,000.

Now the road is usually host to a lot of parked cars. The houses look freshly painted and well kept.

This very faded photograph is of the Villa on the River Wye bank at Hunderton. The sign shows that they sold Hereford Brewery Ales and Stout. A popular river trip from here would have been up to Breinton Springs.

The buildings are virtually unchanged but the ferry steps have been lost in the undergrowth. The bank mooring has a raft awaiting next year's rafters race.

The Boys House of St Elizabeth School Bullingham. It was possibly the largest elementary boarding school in Hereford and was run by the Sisters of Charity of St Vincents de Paul, originally from their chief house in Paris. The buildings comprised a home for the sisters, St Elizabeth House founded in 1860, and an adjoining chapel which was built in 1905.

The outbuilding on the left is being converted into a private house. The main building, although in good repair, is now empty. Its future is unknown.

Rotherwas Hall about 1906. This was a large stately home only just outside the City which was occupied by Count Louis Bodenham-Lubienski (d. 1909). It was built in 1731 on the site of an earlier mansion and the hall contained some very fine oak carvings taken from the older house. The old chimney was dated 1613. The estate included 1,628 acres of land as well as 36 of water, and was sold on September 5th 1912 by Edwards, Russell and Baldwin. Some of the panelling is now incorporated into Amherst College, Massachussetts, USA. The house was finally demolished in 1925.

The house was partly destroyed in a fire on January 7th 1909 and later demolished. All that can be seen is the earthen bank where the house once stood. In the background is Rotherwas Chapel, now disused, but listed as an ancient monument. The field is now tended by its owners, brothers K. and A. R. Goodwin. The photo was taken with their kind permission.

This postcard of a small terraced house in Green Street was posted on 21st July 1915. The residents, a mother and her two children with the family dog, pose for the photographer — perhaps the father.

The street numbers have changed and the author had a problem identifying the house. However, the detective work paid off when this house was found. It has been altered out of all recognition and awaits a purchaser at £54,000. It has two bedrooms. I wonder what future generations will think of the alterations. By the way, it is the house on the right!

Litley Court was the centre of a large Victorian estate, which was sold at auction in many lots by auctioneer Mr. Edwin Stooke on 7th September 1877. One house on the estate was called Drayton House, later renamed Plas Gwyn, which was to become the home of Sir Edward Elgar. Litley Court was resold in 1884 when it had only 32 acres.

Today the house, now occupied by the Ministry of Agriculture, Fisheries and Food, retains only its immediate surrounding land. A large housing estate is now in the adjacent field. The trees have almost closed the view from the river and the photograph had to be taken some way up stream to get a glimpse of the house. The people in the inflatable craft are on low water and unable to see the house.

Plans for the new Garden City Estate in Hereford, following closely the principles of Ebenezer Howard at Letchworth and Welwyn Garden City, were put forward by Fred Bulmer at a meeting in the Town Hall in 1908. Hereford Co-operative Housing Ltd. was launched on ground from the former Penn Grove Estate. The names of the Bulmer family are found on the street signs. Tenants could become shareholders of the company by paying a small weekly subscription. By the Second World War all the land had been built on and the loans nearly re-paid. The postcard is dated 1915.

The view today along Bulmer Avenue shows that the houses are unchanged on the outside but trees are mature. The inside of the houses have been modernised. They are of different sizes and designs to suit the requirements of applicants.

Ladies Training College, Hereford.

The Ladies Training College Hereford about 1910. The buildings were erected in 1880 in the style of the Victorian Gothic revival, complete with narrow ecclesiastical windows and a central tower. It was originally a boys' school under the management of a limited company but it was not a success and wound up in 1903, when it was put up for sale. The Hereford Times described it as a white elephant.

The buildings are now occupied by the Royal National College for the Blind, founded in 1872, which moved to Hereford on October 1st 1978, and is famous for being the only college of its kind in the world. It trains only the able visually impaired people for open employment and university entrance. The new building to the right is the piano tuning and repairs department. Note the window alterations on the left side.

The Hereford Training College library about 1914. The Old Boys College used this room as a chapel and the main structural features remain. Here it is used as a library, though the number of books seems rather low. The large leaded windows allow a good natural light into the room. In 1904 the Old Boys College was purchased by the Herefordshire Education Committee for £8,500 with some financial help from the City Council and it became the first Local Education Authority Teachers Training College to be opened in the country. After advertising the opening of a two year course, 560 applications were received for the first 50 vacancies. The maximum number of students at the start of the second year was 104. The appointed Principal was Miss Sophie Smith.

The room is now used by the Royal National College for the Blind as a recital room. It has been visited by Royalty and many world famous musicians. The Principal is Lance Marshall, M.A., Dip.Ed., F.B.I.M. and its President The Rt. Hon. the Lord Howard de Walden T.D.

COX'S COTTAGE, VENNS LANE

The cottage in Venns Lane — a postcard dated 1905 shows its occupant watching the photographer. It was lived in by the famous Victorian water colour artist David Cox 1783-1859 for some years while he taught art at the Academy for Young Ladies, now the Farmers Club, in Widemarsh Street. Note the window which has been bricked in above the entrance porch.

About 20 years ago the road was widened and the stone wall erected. The roof was re-thatched in 1987 with imported french reeds. The thatcher was confident that they would last for over 80 years. The cottage is now a listed grade II building, and hopefully a missing wall plaque will be replaced.

List of Places and Events

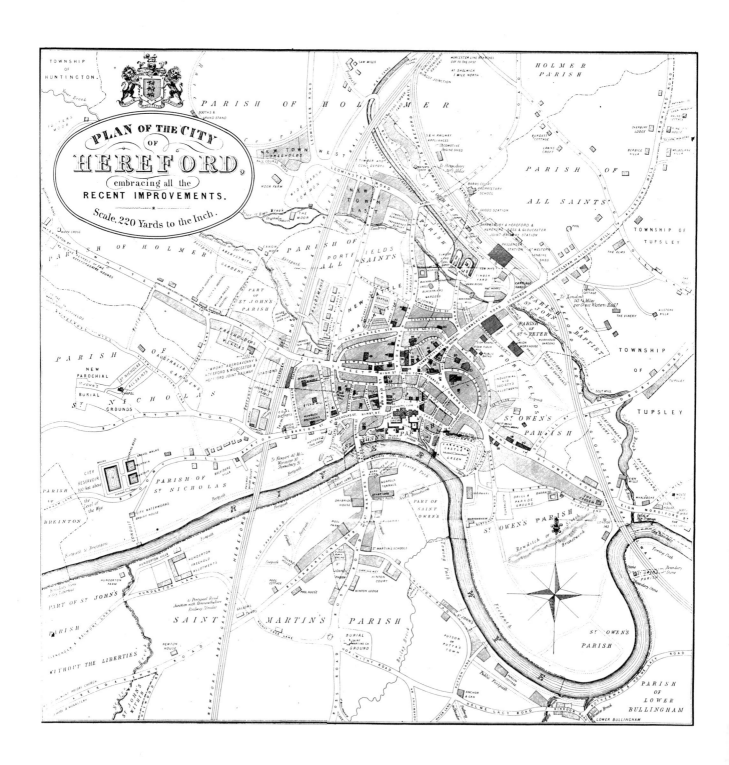